Challiwimbe N'Goto was born ii
the University of Muzazala, maj
The author's first work in the En
of 'The Book of Times', the c
and hyperbole. Roundly ˌ
charities, N'Goto was seminal in setting up the B'tata
Deforestation Plantation, where bush urchins farm the
imperiled twanza tree for firewood sixteen hours a day
(half day off for Harvest Festival). Challiwimbe's works
remain in print internationally wherever there is
an internet connection and a printer with ink.

Verito Humour

'Guardianista! Trolling the Self-Righteous – a book of good humour'

This book is proudly written in Britisher English. Savour the
flavour man! You can taste the words as little fruits from
the bush – sweet on the tongue like a fresh lady.

This book is a work of parody, caricature and review.
Available in the United Kingdom.

ISBN-13: 978-1530943128
ISBN-10: 1530943124

Guardianista!

- Trolling the Self-Righteous -

a book of good humour

by

CHALLIWIMBE N'GOTO

ZAITA

PROVINCE OF THE FREE

Contents

FIRST THINGS

You can lead the Guardian man to the water, but you cannot pull the stick out of his back end. A team of stumpy Bushmen, strong like hippos but more ugly, may try but fail. Do not waste your energy – save it already: the green way is the modern way! Let him keep it up there, no sweat.

One big thing to know of the Guardian person is they come in three flavours: man, woman, and GBLT. The last one of these is the new one, and is easy to remember if you like the bacon, lettuce and tomato sandwich in your belly. ('G' is for 'granary' in this mnemonicization.) You have to walk carefully on their terrains, like a vole in fear of the cheetah. They like to spring out from behind a bush to scare you with their big roaring speech agendas. I have sometime been made to critic for my spelling of words by the Guardian readermen/women/other-types. This I will not accept from colonial oppressives in their big ivory mansions of the North, builded brick by brick by my ancestors' own crying hands. Desist man! Do not bite the fingers that make your T-shirts cheap.

At the same time I have got big benefits from the

Technology Of The Northmen. So I say thankyou for the smartsphone, for all the joys it's bringing – who can live without it, I ask in all honestness? Thank you for my Grundig, for giving it to me. And my satellite box (of Matsui).

Apart from that everything is rubbish here in Zaita. My room where I stay in the week is so small there is hardly enough space to swing a stick for beating the dog, like we say. (Lucky for me I have no dog. Phew!) I can blame this small room directly to the factory manager who is from Belgium and made a deliberate bad design on the accommodations. When you light the briar there is no way for smoke to go out and the fishmeat smell makes the next door man come and beat me with his fists (no room for stick, remember – small mercy result!). One day I will travel into Belgium and become an architect of revenge. In the meandays I am to migrate soon by Britain, for my online wife is Scots woman who has a full passport under her tartan hat. She is a very nice lady who sends me money for an operation for my sister (who is me in a wig). I am learning much from her vocabulations on webchat, and in reading of the Guardian, so I can make best preparations for assimilating in the easy way – like a cultural camel-lion. Interact and learn: it's the new way man! Blessings upon the Chairman of Grundig. Through him I can make my big leap forward into the 20th century. It is all done web-style!

TOLERATIONS

You can put up with anyone if you try. Guardian man (or person) is always very tolerant of all other peoples (or persons) who are in agreement with him (or her, or ... um). This is the new way of the world – you cannot beat a man around the head simply because he made a vote for the other party or you disagree with his stupid thoughtpoint. You must stay civil and make a pen your weapon instead of the machete. This is now done on the 'net from behind the moat of the British castlehouse, where the Guardian commenter types angry words and gets a disease in the spleen. Sometimes the head explodes too (metaphor, I expect). Small price for him.

I always like to take a long walk before making my web comment as it serves to cool down the head nice. Or by the alternative way, it is very therapeutic to tenderize goat meat with a hammer for half an hour while my brain does the thinking. Then I can come back to my Grundig and hit my target precisely, like a drone missile on a chimp. After that I return to slaughter my goat – by the neck, swift and humane. (You see how I learn! So much is available on the line nowadays.) But let me make no more ado now, here comes my stuff from copy and paste.

"Dave Grohl writes to Cornwall council to allow local band to practise"

This is a story of a music group who nobody likes ('Black Leaves of Envy') who were writing to Mister Grohl of the popular Foo Fighters band because of idiot Cornish noises restriction that was stopping them making their noises in Cornland. I was made to wonder if Mister Grohl might help Challi too. You can see comments below this.

challi: I am to come and sit outside Grohl front door and bang my chassanga in the morning and the noon and also the night time. It makes a nice noise like a spakkawatta being eaten by a sallooboa. This he will like most greatly because I have perfected the art. Big up support for Zaita Music. Thank you in advances Mister Grohl for your kind amenities towards upcoming talents of which I am integral partition. Adele can move over.

bugsy: Doubtless there are plenty of hapless goons like yourself pestering Dave Grohl day and night with supposed 'tunes' rendered on djembe drums and skulls.

challi: You can indeed make a very good sound with the skull. Antilope is good. Or go to nearest mass-grave and choose the best one with not much damage. Leave to dry in sun, then peel and core (we say 'brainscoop'). Sand it off, and if you are posh you may lacquer down with chicken grease. For best noise you will need a stick – about a footlength – on which you bind a stone at one end. Now you are ready to go. (By complete chance my favourite own head-drum is of Ottu, my old neighbour from down the road who got a successful lynch in the uprising[†]. What is this chance!?!) For best result, hit on the part just above the forehead. Whack it man!

bugsy: You are sick.

challi: Unless you are a professional doctor madam I suggest you keep this diagnosis for yourself – in the end where the birds don't sing.

[†]True comicdote: With my musical percussions I was onetime able to woo the old widow of Ottu. This was with a beautiful bang-along to a traditional Zaita romantic courting song ("Oh come and play now, my fruit is bursting"). She is a little past her best at 17 but experience makes up for this one – Ottu was her third husband and she knows the tricks up her sleeve. I made a very good job on her and was back in time for Match of Day on Matsui. She will never know how Ottu's own head made her mine!

<u>wardy3</u>: The Foos are a top band. Keep rocking Black Leaves of Envy. Crank it up!

<u>challi</u>: Help please me wardy3! I have a REALLY good metal band but get troubles from neighbours who like to always complain. I must make a move. Where do you live? I need to move to a tolerant and diverse neighbourhood where I do not get predjudiced against my good music. Send me postcode and I can relocate exactly your way. Great blessings to you for your love and understanding of the BEST METAL MUSIC!

<u>warden3</u>: Righto. And what kind of metal do you play?

<u>challi</u>: Mostly I use pipes, old oil drums, and corrugated roofing on top of neighbour's house. You can play all day there in the sun.

<u>warden3</u>: Get lost.

As you can learn from above, one of biggest intolerances making a blight on the countries of the world is against the foreigners (you call them refugers). I have big feelings as you see in the next one coming up ahead of you.

"Migration is a fact of life – yet our deluded leaders try to turn back the tide"

This was a 'piece' (journalister slang) by a lady called Simon Jenkins. Well as you may know, immigrants are a subject close to my own belly. But I do not like the Guardian column to insult me by this speak of a 'tide'. I am not water, I am not fish, I am indeed a human, which as every Guardianer knows is a kind of person. And one day I have a big hope to make the move your way (I talk to you, Britishers!) because I have made the great web-friendliness of a lady of the Scottish Lands who I wish to take as my wife to become. I call her my online wife because she has made kindness to me over a Skype line (detail is private but let me only say you can get a lot even from a small Grundig). This type of ceremony – marriage consumption – is legal-binding here. She made me very encouraged and I could not help to put a comment on this story in case UK government was reading.

challi: I can come now with family too. I have useful skills and can make the call of any bird to attract one my way. Then I capture her and make very good roast with secret herb recipy of my best aunt Nettie. She can come too because she is the normal cook of our house with fried sheep eye speciality. If this is new for you

you can learn from us. Exchange the difference!

<u>friendofafriend</u>: Quaint. Any more words of 'wisdom'?

<u>challi</u>: Indeed yes. I myself have made a learning from you guys: I was once introducted to a very polite Englishman who made a big impression when I was to shake his hand. 'Lovely as it is to welcome our multicultural brethren,' he said with a wise look on his face, 'I maintain that one should never shake the hand of anybody unacquainted with the high water mark of civilization that is lavatory paper. Good day to you!' I never did get to shake his hand, but his words of good education have remained with me, and to this day I make a special point to use paper*. So to Madam Jenkins, the articulator of this article, I say please open your home to me. I am knocking in a metaphor on your window through this comment so that I may share in your riches. I will work for my upkeeps. Am I not blessed with two hands and good teeth? I can tear the top off a pineapple with my strong jaw! I say again, open up! Else I will huff and puff and blow down your door. (I have good lungs.)

At this point of writing I am still awaiting to hear from your governing ministrations. Get it a move on man!

*Subjecting to availability.

13

"Northern Ireland bakers guilty of discrimination over gay marriage cake"

This one here was a very righton articulation about a bakerman and his ladywife who would not make a gay cake with slogans. It was to have popular characters Bert and Ernie on it, who were the first ever TV gaypals.

challi: 8 articles on this site today about one cake! And no mention of copyright infringing. I know you western types: Sesame Street legal action soon no doubt.

sheppybush: It's not really about cake though, right?

challi: Please try to tell my original wife this. She has now been making talk about cake all day since reading these articles here. Tomorrow I am off to buy her cake stuff but must walk seven mile to town for this where there is new 'mall' market. (This is a repressive westernism. You cannot even buy yamyam or juice of the twanza fruit, only American chip bags and fizzcans of cola.)

sheppybush: What an odd person you are. Concerned about the rights of two felt TV characters yet intolerant of two sentient human beings who wished only to buy a cake?

<u>challi</u>: Indeed madam I do not express intolerance, I am in actual-life half gay for myself (it is my right hand that is the glad one) – and also married (watch this space however). I focus on cake as I am keen to learn your baking styles (by eating, not cooking, as I already say I have a cookwife). Please read the Book of Times, wherein you will learn that,

"He who is righteous unto others and he who is righteous unto himself shall by those who are themselves righteous unto any man be judged in the same mouth of air as one and the same, and so shall they come by the wisdom of inheritance through the path of verity, illuminated by the light of oneness that doth shine down upon those of good mind and deed so the man of dancing heart may reveal himself to the world as the heir to the blessings rightly bestowed upon those who haven entered the time of being and the space of knowing bearing with them the gifts of life rendered unto them alone by This Book of worldly learnings wherein these pearls may themselves be apprehended by he who is of fair heart and upon whom the earthly burden doth fall lightly, for shall not the truth be found to echo in the ears of he whose eyes are wide to its wisdoms so that the goodly words therein may forevermore be elevated in the blissness of one, whether it be the rainy season or not?"

Maybe you can learn a little from us in the big world today? This is a leaf you can take from my book – if you give me an address I can post the page rightaway.

I await on you eagerly, Challi.

Despite my kind offer I was never to hear back from this rude man. But I would not be deterred with my tolerations of ignorance. In Guardianland and wider Britannia one must show respect for all types, not just people of different genital orientation, as you will see in the next articule.

"People with dwarfism deserve respect – not ridicule"

This was a strong opinionated piece about a night club in Manchester that was giving special midget people to their VIP visitor people. Although it is a very funny story it is no laughing matter. (If you have to do it make a small chuckle on the inside so nobody notice, or wait until no one is looking at you and let it go bigtime. Respect always!)

challi: We must not take it out on the small persons! Pity on them with they little winkles. Make a pick on somebody your own size – I say this as one who is well above the average ;-). Useful point: my friend Wollo has stilts for help as he has only half legs. DON THEM MAN! You can move real quick.

groovinon: I'm sure that will go down well with the marginalized for whom this article speaks. If you have any further advice please be sure to keep it to yourself.

challi: I do not presume to act your advisor sir/madam/other. I will leave you only with this one bad happening – when I was made to suffer from an attack of a group of 'dwarves' as you call it (we say 'pygmy' or 'desert critter'). They caught me out in a field and beat my legs with sticks. There is good and bad everywhere and it does not matter how tall you are, this we know from always. Apprehend however that the chant of my attackers was "Break the evil long-legs." I will not tolerate these prejudices in this day of age when I am going about my private business hunting the hare on their stupid sacred land. It was a terrible thing to be in this persecuted minority of one! Lucky I got only bruises because I was able to kick out good and hard. I made a nice defence and broke two heads quite well. Caught a big hare that day too. Silver lining for me.

Groovinon: What the **** are you on (about)?

The asterixes are from me there. It is bad language like that that makes me to think twice about my migrating in the UK. Hopefully your tongues are more civilize than your writing. I never hear a swearword from Gary Linekers.

PROGRESSIVE POLITICALS

Guardian Person is always playing on their harp about 'progressive'. You will see this in their columns and in their free-comments: "You must make the progressive policies", "This is the progressivist way", "We must do the progressions", and "The contrast of post-marxist and pseudo-homogenous dialectics cannot be observed subjectively within the metacontrarian view of empirical feminism per se – leading to parallels, or sub-parallels, with the non-didactic discourse concerning a neo-libertarian context seen as a preobjective truth."

This is to mean that it is my way or the high way – and no mistakes or else. Nietzsche was a bigtime progressive. So was Stalin. And definitely any businessperson who says 'going forwards' at the beginning of their sentences. (Sidenote however: progressive rock 'n' roll – 'progrocks' – is very backwards. How can you make progress if you go backward?) Now you can see easy: because this 'progressive' does not mean too much, you can use this word a lot to make yourself sound good to stupids. Result for me! Now I have a manifesto (I call this The Challifesto):

Going ahead into the future that lies before us, I am to be a progressive kind of progressive, one who will make forward progress. This is the new progressiveness; the fifth way! Onwards, brothers and sisters – and granary sandwich munchers.

"There is a vision of what a progressive Britain could be. It's called Canada"

This is where someone who lives in one country makes a big complain that their country (UK) is not like another country that they like better than the one that they live in. There is only one country in the world that does not do this and that is Canada – because it is the best country in the world. This is given a good explaining in the Guardian: it is no small thank you to its grand hero president Mister Trudeau, who has solved all the problems of the world that exist there. There was not much to say about this in my comment but it was important to make big my 'progressive credentials' with a bold statement:

challi: Britain, step into the future. This is not 1950! You can be progressive too. Put your best foot onwards and move into the progression with a step in the forward direction. To do this first you must be goodTHINKING – which will lead to goodACTing. You need to make everyone equal to everybody else even if they do not have the natural ableness in an inequitable worldspace. Ride the wave of Trudeau and cure your dystopia. Make it happen buddy!

Nobody made a reply because my comment was quickly 'moderated'. (This is efficiency system where the Guardian edit-heads select only the best parts of your contribution – cutting my 75 words down to 0 – so it makes more sense.) As you must imagine, I was truly blessed already to have an editor assigned to my work after only two days on the site!

"Knives are out for Jacob Zuma as South Africa's Guptagate grows"

I felt compulstion to express my progressive view point in this – as you will sorely appreciate. Mister Zuma is a hero very much in my chest.

challi: The knives are a very bad method on 'Zumaman', as we call him. In this day and age of humanity you can do better by the electric chair. Embrace the technology to show the world we are not the backward kind. For heaven's sake man this is the twenty–first century and no man or woman should be put at the sword! Think to Saudi House wherein the knifeman is still active. Nuclear power generator – get it now for secure future supply. Sparks can fly forever on the crooks!

mattyquick: Just when I thought the bounds of idiocy had been reached, some dunderhead manages to chip in with this. How anyone could take 'knives out' so literally is beyond me ... Get back to school.

challi: My school was best for educates, sir, not indoctrinates like in UK system. We are to think for ourself and make our own interprets. If you try to make an idiot suggestion on the rear end of my face then you fail because I understand your Englander backhand humour but do not respond in the same kind. I take the high ground and tell you to go stick your own 'chip in' at the other end where the potatos go out not in.

This time my comments were allow to stay – my effort to do a polite chat had clearly been made appreciated.

"Scottish referendum explained for non-Brits"

This was the big devolutionistics debate where the downtrodden peoples of Scotland ('Scots') decided to stay under the hefty foots of your lady-Queen and keep calling themself 'Britishers'.

glasgowkiss: People who refer to themselves as 'British' need boiling.

challi: Boiling someone can work as a general punishment, but for describing a countryperson it is very harsh! I have seen boiled heads in the traditional shrunken style. Let us say indeed that the perpetrator does not commit the crime the second time after such punishment (British would insert smileface here). My aunt's husband was headboiled for his big sin but the killing of the guilty happens before by efficient method so dignity of criminal is kept.

andypandy: "My aunt's husband was headboiled" ... I really can't tell whether you're serious.

Challi: Like we say Andy, you cannot dance on the

trampoline while you make your knitting – for therein lies the path to blindness. It is the same for the beasts of the field, among whom sheep number.

<u>andypandy</u>: Er. I expect you boil the sheep too ...?

<u>challi</u>: Two thumbs up you madam for your grand idea, however I do not have a big enough pot.

"Cologne attacks: we must avoid the risk of 'sexual jihad'"

This is an article in which, after some outlanders made unrequited love-advances on indigenous populations of the Teutonicalsbundeslande, the very brain-headed writer Mister White was explaining, "mutual tolerance and some good luck should see all sides' experience of the refugee crisis through a period of adjustment".

<u>challi</u>: You simply cannot argue with the brighthood of this articulate. I have a VERY nice recipy for the good luck you are making a demand of. First you take a bark of a Junzubo plant (rough translate is, 'the bush that has no name and grows in the land of the unknown in the time of the future to come') and dry it in the sun of the middle day of the middle month of the middle year. Then do a good pulverizing of it with stones from the Cave Of No Return (turn left at Zaita lake and follow signs). This powder you have now must be mixed with the milk of a billygoat and the grinded horns of a sea frog until you have a paste of purest brown (gooey colour). Smear this ALL over your face – DO NOT LEAVE OUT FOREHEAD – and make a proper nice dance at the correct hour on the correct day of

the correct month of the correct year (which is 1928 – BC not AD, do not get it wrong way round or luck will be bad). You must carry a Beatbox tuned to Radio Coolbeat 96.7 ('where the party goes on 24/7') and remember to wear a green feather by your ear as you make your wish. For this you will get very BEST luck – there is no other way for this – and your Europa 'refugee crisis issue' will be COMPLETELY solutioned (you can also say solutionized if you are of better educates). Welcome to Utopia!

Again there was some very ingenious moderating of my words and I did not get any printable replies for your pleasure – but as you will see, Challi is a fast learnerman: step your face into the next section.

DIFFERENTIALS

It is nice to explore the differings between cultures of different types. Guardian community of commentors is like a little village – only a VERY DIVERSE little village where all the village idiots like to share their opinionations for all to benefit. For me if I get the outsider view I can learn, like the alien spaceman who came to visit Area 51. We all must 'challenge the worldviews' like you say. Even if sometime UK problems can seem funny to us – like having wrong colour yoga mat so you must see the therapy doctor to fix your head. (I can fix quicker with one metal pipe, you soon forget about yoga – this is one joy where you can learn from us too. Give and take, yes?) So here I like to explore the tiny differences that make our culture-features unique – like you have umbrella and we have parasol (ha-ha!).

When in engagement with a new culture, however, remember this one thing of big importance: you cannot even begin if your mind is all clutter-up with thoughts – or even worse, prejudices. Always start with an open head and an empty brain. See you on the other side of here.

"Modern rail travel is a slow-grinding nightmare of too many people and too little space"

I read of your many rail-problems which are to include the leaves and the snow and the lazy driver. Now you have overcrowding riots where the police must come in and clear the extra passengers out with their truncheons.

challi: Typical First World's Problem made from nothing! If there is a space 'issue' in the carriage berth I always take to use the roof. Only a few people there and nice breeze to cool it down good. You guys can get your traditional orange face. Relax dude!

valderama: Might be OK in India but not here mate.

challi: You can learn a little from us too friend: best advice to stay on last truck so to avoid hot steam in face. You can make a nice BBQ there and enjoy. My current wife is wheelchairbinded (I use string for safety purpose) but if we come to your UK, idiot 'accessible' rules cannot allow her on roof. Discrimination man! You need liberty for disableds and you need it now. You can't always get Molly to coddle them. Come into the 21st century, you are welcome.

"Channel 4's Benefits Street returns with nearly 3 million viewers"

This was about a television programme on the fantastic Channel 4 (read more in my Sporting section later). It is all about the poor persons of Britain who cannot do any work because of their bad spines.

challi: I can not bring myself to watch this programming – two reasonings: 1, Pain of seeing fall of England and poverty of starving. 2, Dam Matsui stop working last night. Better I think send money to your charity. Which is best to help starving? I can send online.

northernlights: Nepal Earthquake Appeal.

lifeonmars: Why not spend it on English lessons?

challi: I take many English lessons already. Because someone is not perfect in a language it is not for you to ignore. You make better use of you time to respond to comment instead of insulting person who makes much admirings for your country. Indeed my new wife (almost wife) is also Scottish lady. Shame on yours.

lifeonmars: Thank you for your reply. If you wish to be understood better, it would however be helpful to improve your English a little. Still I'm sure it's better than my ... whatever your native language is. Worth noting that the Scottish wife is not pertinent – unless you view her as some kind of trophy, which would be impolite at best.

challi: Indeed my wife will be a fine trophy! Many would be proud to have her for their biddings – as it shall come to pass if I can make a migration your way. But my real subject was to where can I send monies for your charities of UK hungry and poverty situation?

petespeaks: Go jump in the lake.

challi: I hear this expression several times from before – must be difficult British humour, like "break a leg". Or maybe not. Perhaps a nice invitation to go swimming in the Park of Regents lake?

petespeaks: Just jump.

challi: ... Up and down?

"Bear Grylls show accused of 'callous disregard for life' as 450 complain"

Vegetariablism is one big cultural difference between here and you. No matter how hard you look you will not find the vegetarians here: they have been beat into hiding. Really it is compulsory to eat the meat every day. If the market is closed you must eat your Grandma. (Joke! Meat is too old and tough.) Serious though, man: meat is good for your brain and brings luck to your belly. In this TV programme of the article, many softhead Englanders were made to complain about the slicing of pig throats on their televisions. In Zaita culture there is not much difference between a vegetable and an animal, which is really a type of fruit with horns.

rubytwo: What do people think meat is made from? It doesn't grown on trees, does it.

challi: Sir, let me please inform you that it is made from particles of dead animal. From the tree is coming the nuts. This is the isolated living of small island of Great Britain where your meat come in pacquets from supermark and factory process line. Come to visit and we shall kill animals by the neck together under the sun without a roof and chew the bark of the twanza tree as friends.

<u>rubytwo</u>: Erm, you're not selling it very well.

<u>challi</u>: Come I say, and we will feast the feast of kings! I shall prepare a banquet and we will perform the ceremony of Shattamawanga by eating each other's kidneys. There is no higher honour in my land.

<u>tomgonewrong</u>: As a carnivore who has slaughtered his own food I must say that careful steps should be – and are – taken to minimise the suffering of the animal. The methods employed in this programme, however, are thoroughly barbaric.

<u>challi</u>: Tomgonewrong, first thing to realize is that you do not have to kill the beast. If I am feeling peckish on a Tuesday lunchtime I am often to sneak into the farmer's field and take the two delicacies from under a goat with my bolt cutter. Good to tide you over until dinner – and a laugh to look on his confusing face after (I mean now the goat, not the farmer). Second thing: if you do not like this Mister Grills, I suggest you wait for next uprising to do your move. You have the training and tools for to make a proper chop-up job on him. (If you can post the skull I will add to my percussion set.)

"Budget 2016 live: Osborne hails 'sugar tax' on soft drinks but cuts growth forecasts"

This was the Great Sugar Tax Reform of 2016 – to make fat Britishers slim again. This is how you can lose weight from only sitting in your chair with the remote control. It is just one great example of the world-known British Innovation.

challi: We like to say that there are many ways to skin the bushman, which is to say there are many ways to take your taxes. Problem is you use them ALL. Best to make one rate of tax on all things – you can even liberate your accountants to make better use of them in the fields where man is happy herding the beasts.

trickymicky: 'many ways to skin the bushman' ... Does the bushman have anything to say in all this?

challi: Of course not Mister Mickey! He does not speak because he is dead (by very quick method with no sweat broken). For skinning, I prefer the cut starting on the ankles, followed by pulling. It is hard work but with a good reward, but always take careful not to strain your muscle because the Bushman is a tough customer pal.

<u>lazybones</u>: So while disabled people accept vicious cuts, the headline's about some dumb sugar tax?!

<u>challi</u>: This is terrible. Do not make vicious cuts on your disables! This must be a police action. Where do you make the chop on them? ... Disabled are a subject in my own head also – my outgoing wife is herself in a wheelchair, and my cousin Yongu has epileptics (he is very sensible of loud noises or car flashing lights when he is driving the bus).

"The truth about poo: we're doing it wrong"

This was by a clever microbiology lady who thinks she can teach this old dog new toilet tricks. Think again woman!

challi: We have a saying from which the world can learn: do not make a turd in your own river, rather make it in the river of your enemy, for the bad man will get his just reward when he goes fishing.

missthetrain: Wise words mate.

challi: Indeed one of best parts of life is to make excretions in the bush, which is daily pleasure for me. The Bush People do not mind too much. For ablutions after one can not beat the leafs of the twanza tree if handy. They are soft and you can chew to get high (not after usings please).

missthetrain: Charming!

challi: Madam we cannot afford your luxuries here. When I was a worker at the international hotel I was fond to use old copy of the Guardian (opinions section) but paper is quite rough. Make it softer, I beg on you.

-ISMS & EQUALITIES

The Guardian column people like to play a game I call 'Colonel Sander and Uncle Ben'. They can look at a baked bean on their plate and see a 'race issue' (a.k.a. racialism in anybody's book you like). They can make a living out of GBLT – but if they wake up with one in their bed, they run like a mountain dog with a firework in the back end. (This is a fact: when I work as porter in old Empire Hotel – called now New Freetown Hotel – I find one Britisher who wants Guardian paper in the room for morning reading. In true-proof experiment, I unlock her door early and climb into bed dressed like Grayson Izzard – with white face and a *very* nice dress from my Aunt Nettie. If I say so myself, I was looking quite a good sight when it is all considered. Then, as I lie there with small grin on my face, I slowly poke her til she wake. Like the manager says, this is "above and beyond the calling of duty", and after that I do not work so much on the customer services side. This manager is also from Belgium and everybody know they are all racial there anyway so you can not win. It is everywhere these days.)

Other isms are sexism and ageism and feminism. One

thing that is big to remember, however, is that all isms are equal. If you think one ism is more important than another ism, then you are what is called an ism-ist. This is the worst kind of 'ist' ... at least sort of – because it ism-ism is of course *equal* worst with all the others. Equality is here to stay man! I hope you have the knack of it enough to go onwards now.

"Kick It Out needs helping out if football is truly serious about fighting racism"

The was a story about giving money to the anti-racism party, which you simply can not make an argument against. As a half Afro-Caribbean (I am just the Afro part), I naturalistically have sentimentalities on this. There was a video by the column of an Arsenal supporter lady (also known as a 'goonie') making a nasty chant-up against the Tottenhammers: "I've got a foreskin – haven't you, you barmy Jew?" This was very rude and they want to Kick It Out.

tottenman: A woman with a foreskin? ... That's Arsenal fans for you.

challi: I have one from bygones that I keep in a special glass box. Sometimes I put it inside the refridgerator to frighten my wife.

smarties78: Are they truly serious about kicking it out? High time something was actually done.

challi: If you can hold the racist to the floor you can try to kick it out of him (or her) but I do not think this is a very nice way to proceed in the modern day. When we see a person we disagree with we find it best to tell the police.

Smarties78: ... you call the police just because someone doesn't agree with you?

challi: This is why we pay them for man! Then they can take him to the back of the enclosure and do the kicking on our behalf. It is the modern way – by the book not the crook as we say. (Only make bruise not blood, you cannot tell after two weeks. Never to face or private area.) Alternative is the waterboard which leaves no mark – wash the racism out!

"Middle-class feminism has a blind spot over female cleaners"

This was an article complaining that there are too many poor-class ladies working as cleaner ladies for classy ladies.

challi: This is not 2015. Get contemporary dude! We do not have your social problems at home. Women of any class can always get good work on the binround like we have them here – the overalls are free when you sign up with the manager, who is also a lady. Come into the new way – we in the wide world are ready to embrace you with our arms and our hearts open whatEVER your class or gender bias. (We have room for GBLT too – the rate for a 15-minute try is very fair indeed.) No need to be the smallhead in these matters.

loveman: Hmm. You sound like a thoroughly modern chap.

challi: Thanks for appreciating. Note it is always best to get a strong one with good stay-power to do the cleaning – healthy and not too fat so they can get it done quick and get out. You do not want to see them bending over and making a sight while you try to eat your lunch. I do interviews in the yard – test fitness with press-ups followed by a small race. Winner gets the job. I do not run a charity but I give a very nice bonus. Earn it mate!

loveman: So tell us, how much do you shell out for your cleaners??

challi: Normal is two pounds of kudu.

loveman: I have no idea what that amounts to … exchange rate?

challi: No man, kudu is meat of the antilope – you can take doe or buck, we are not sexualist about it. No slaughter so OK for vegetarian people too.

loveman: ?!?

challi: Just chop a lump off the hind part – grows back in three months.

"Love wins: Guardian marriage equality forum feels the passion"

I could not understand this story at all but it was important to make a good comment on it so I would not look stupid.

challi: I always make a big support for the female lesbians among the world. At the same time no lady should be made compulsion to be one. You can take the horse to the water hole but you cannot make her drink. Do not force it buddy!

fairfilly: wtf?

challi: No need for this obscuring – make an elaboration man if you want to be understand!

"Why cast a lighter-skinned actor as Nina Simone? Here come the racesplainers"

This is an article by Guardian's own Minister for Racism and Inequals, who was making the big point that the problem in filming is not the person infront of the camera (lady called Saldana) but the person behind it (called the 'cameraperson'). There was talking of whether the actor lady's nose was the right shape and colour and a very big discussion on this with the commenters:

challi: In the time of Nina Simone we had black and white television. (Almost no man had colour.) Make the film in black and white and the problem is reduced a little, no?

ageofreason: Yep, reckon you've got it all sorted there. I'm sure everyone's happy with that solution.

challi: Thank you for supporting. Saldana has pretty small nose I say, so nose makeup IS necessary to make the nose more big like Lady Nina's conker. Also the actress has nice long straight hairs, different to the short curlies of Nina. I want to see this film anyway because Miss Simone sings beautiful like a dog of the plains. You can kiss the sound!

ageofreason: I guess you're the kind of guy who'd be OK with a black actor 'whiting up' for a white part?

challi: No problem man. Cate Blanchett would make a nice Nina because she is a top-time actress with a real good nose. Fact also on your subject is that Ronnie McDonald is a blackman with whitepaint face. This you can put in your gourd for smoking on a thoughtful one.

"When I'm 64, I'll still be singing along"

Another day, another ism! This was the blatant ageism in the Beatles song 'When I Am Sixty-Four' with its "negative portrait of ageing" that the paper made a highlight on.

geoman: Amid all this surrealism surrounding a simple pop song are we not ignoring society's failings and merely chasing pipe dreams?

challi: Sir(?), I know exactly what you mean about chasing pipe dreams. I had one just the same. I was outside in the dark, running after a lorry that I could not seem to catch, no matter how hard I pushed myself – yet the lorry was only going slowly(!). It was a flatback style vehicle, and on the back, secured (after a fashion!) with a few ropes lay – you have guessed it – a pipe. It was of medium length (maybe three metres), possibly formed of fired clay, but quite wide (two metres?) and of a type suitable for sewage ... I am eager to learn what your pipe was like (this is no innuendo please) in the dream, and the lorry too. Maybe we had the same dream at the same hour? It could be a portent.

geoman: Can you guess where to stick your dream?

GOOD HUMOURS

Like you see, Guardian commenter people do not take to joking, for always someone must be the butt end of this funny business – and they will not make a laugh on anyone, especially themself. Their face goes serious strange like the newscasterman (before the nice story at the end with a dog stuck in a hole made free by ten firepeople) and then foam comes out from the ears on both sides of the head – just like the experiment we made in school chemistry class with Stoupi Btangi* the bushboy. Consequentials of this is that the Good Humours section of this book must remain empty. Thank you for trying.

*In health and safety you may be surprised we take very serious measures: Mister Cooper who was to administer the chemical took to wearing his safety goggles and we boys of the class were made to stand on other side of the field with fingers in our ears while he lighted the fuse.

Here is a nice picture of artistic merits made by me, Challi, age eleven. Even today I take a very simple pleasure in my enjoyment of this memory.

MISTER
COOPER SIR

STOUP,
BTANG

SODIUM
DOUBLE
PHOSPHATE

GENETICALS &
LADY MATTERS

One must try hard not to be backward on the subject of the ladies – this is 2016 remember, even in China*. I am extremely liberalized when it comes to these matterings and always like to ask before having a go. You can do little things to help too, gentlemen. If your good lady is struggling with the shopping by example, or finding it hard to push your car after a breakdown, a simple shout of encouragement can mean the wide world. Always though try to be sensitive: a plain, "Hurry up now!" is way much more better than a gruff, "Get a b----y move on woman, the big match kicks off in half an hour!"

But it goes on past this my friends. As a modern parent I have been there at the birthing of all my kidlets. Again, there you can howl sweet invigorations in her face – and there will surely be some pretty nurses at hand to make your advance on.

Like you see, here we do not suffer under your western prejudices of other sexes. We will not make so much the emphasise on the looks here – why man, when the wife may be goodlook now but her face will soon go bad and none of your Eurobigots would want her for jiggygogos? We understand the deeper personalities and would make a go on her anyway. Respect gentlemans! Let the donkey be the donkey – do not paint him up like a zebra.

*Correction on myself: it is the year of a monkey in China. They do not have 2016.

"All British women have the right to a caesarean – they're not 'too posh to push'"

Britain is a different country to the world. There you can choose if you want to have your baby like Julius Caesar. Much to think on this one, and when in doubt on genetical matters I like to ask Charles Darwin himself by calling up his spirit in a séance ceremonial. I got a good diviner this time who made some excellent pronouncings to chew at.

<u>challi</u>: With this surgery coming very frequent, you make an evolution issue: the childs of 'narrow-funnel' mothers will get the Caesar Op to survive kid-birth – and will so make a propagating on these geneticals to the next generate. So very quick the small style la-la will become the most common. You may say this is nice for some of us, but the problem becomes that more and more ladypersons will need the Emperor Birth. It will be rife in your hospitals.

<u>ylangylang</u>: The 1900s just phoned. They want you back.

<u>challi</u>: This is a silly comment. The telephone was not in common use then. And nobody has made a time

machine yet. Know your own technologicals chum!

manoftheowls: So instead of birthing by caesarean I should have been left to die to stop my 'bad' genes propagating?

challi: I was only to think on a possible future. By alternative to your Western machete medicine, you can try the Heimlick move – only turn the woman upside down first (and note please there is no need for any actual lick). Or if she is too big to lift you can make a kick on the lower back so it can pop out.

manoftheowls: 'Future'? I think you mean 1750. When you reflect that sub-Saharan Africa has 'evolved' – without the availability of caesareans – to the point that still 5% of women die giving birth, one is bound to observe that your genetic presumption is patently incorrect, not to mention morally questionable. My mother's condition, for the record, was environmental, so I have not inherited it.

challi: Sir, I shall say a little 'hail Caesar' in your honour. You must be very relieve you will not need this painful operation for yourself. If you are of a religious disposal, I heartily apologize.

manoftheowls: I am not even vaguely religious. I am a

doctor, well-versed in cacogenetics, and likely know a good deal more about vaginal accouchement than yourself.

challi: Sir again, I make deference to your bigger knowledge of the v----a (although there was no need for you to brag on this). I know something of them myself – I have a keen layman's interest and have accessorized a good few – but it is always good to get the professional view of a fully-qualified fandango doctor.

manoftheowls: Pardon?

challi: Are you by chance also a winkie physician? There is something I want to show you ...

"Number of British women freezing their eggs soars"

You will not hear of this funny practice here. It is one of the strange habits of the ladies of Britain.

challi: One should not freeze the egg, mostly best to refridgerate for the freeze will impair flavour. If you are to eat them raw – though careful for samonella – you need to leave out to warm for an hour for improved taste. For complements, brown sause is always better than tomato and brown bread better than white (please this is not a racial comment, it is an actual fact that brown tastes better). If you can borrow a car you can fry them on the bonnet – good picnic trick to impress young girl by the woods.

yossaria: Ew. You and some poor defenceless soul?

challi: Au the contrairy sir. You want one with meat on and a good punch. Where I am from, when the sun goes past horizon and the candlesticks go out, the strong lady is our cup of rooibos. But now I must go, for it is nearly sunset and my wife is bellowing.

"Genetic study shows men's height and women's weight drive earning power"

This was a true story to let us know how a man who is 2.5 inches taller of height will earn £1600 more money in the year, while big ladies will earn £3000 less. I was wonderous to how you cannot pay these lovelies more than the thin stress-out ones who are no fun.

challi: As the tallest in my town I was not actually to choose a tall woman for my first wife but a biggie who would immediately say 'yes' (because the tallest in town is most eligible). Other reasoning was that this ample lady could not outrun me in event of escape attempt. (Note: the slimmest woman in our town was Zaita province quickest runner three times over – it has been proofed she can run faster than a flying brick. Check video on YouTube.)

greenfingers: If you are the 'most eligible' I hate to think of the others.

challi: Obvious jealous comment on your part for my big lady! Unfortunate for me now I must tell her to lose twelve kilos quick and inform her boss at the mine of this. With her rise[*] I can afford a 3D television in only ten months, maybe enough left for a visit to massage palace.

stilton: Alan Sugar's only 5 foot something so I don't buy this article.

challi: The diversity in your proud country in respect of Dwarfing Syndrome is to be much admired. We can 'learn a thing or two' from you, as our saying goes. I very much want to be like Mister Sugarman but am much concerned if my tall height will make a prejudice on me(?). Also he may have a big tutoowaa as it is said that the bosspeople are often in possession of these. (I know someone who kept a quanga fruit in the trouser when at work – and was quickly pro-moted.) If I come in England am I to make this kind of embellishing for swift advance up tree?

smarties78: No but you're welcome to a free kick in the balls.

I must say, I love these British humours.

---

[*]Truth is when I confront my wheelie wife with this ultimatum she confess she had lost her digging job already. I tell you she is a lady on borrowtime.

"Women of the world – price equality is in our hands"

This was a very distressing story about pink razors, which cost more money than blue ones in the UK. "We need a revolution to stop such discrimination," the Guardian was telling us, "and ending our complicity is the first step." It seems that the ladies are force-fed to buy the expensive pink ones like in 1984 by Burgess Huxley.

brightstar: When-oh-when will these evil marketing people stop targeting hapless idiots with their cruel pink tricks?

challi: This is non-progressive backwardness! Let the ladies buy blue ones in fairness … Plus I have a big question of dilemma for myself: my wife buys green razors. Where do these lay on the 'marketing spectrum' concerning the man/lady issue? I need to know if she has started moving towards the other side as it is two full moons since our last conjugation and I am becoming suspicious. (I have a new wife in the pipe anyway but this would be good knowledge for future referencing.)

"Teen pregnancy has plummeted. Why do the newspapers never celebrate success?"

This story indeed speaks for itself. Let us make a disco to celebrate and invite the teenage ones who have not yet achieved.

challi: If there will be a party please do not forget to invite me Guardian! When you think on the young ones you must agree that the boy can produce the spermatazo and the girl the egg, so together it will come to pass that they make nature complete – in a most pleasant way indeed! When I see the teenager I think immediately if she is ripe. (A healthy one is good for best.)

simplesample: "She is ripe". Probably the rapiest remark ever in the comments section.

jannos: You need help.

challi: Jannos I have found the help of which you speak! Much Skyping merriment with her last evening (until connection was lost – was compulsed to culminate myself).

"Tampon tax to be scrapped, announces Osborne"

You can see already how the British ladys get to vote in 1975 and now from further campaigns can be made to have Ultimate Freedom with this progression into contemporary living. History will call these liberating ladies The Tamponettes*.

challi: When the goose comes to the gander, you must admire this easing of the levy (not the levee ;-)). It is only fair! In the times of the high churches there were top rate taxes on these things (for moral reasons then) that were to make the world unsanitary – for many ladies deferred to not-wearing, if you can imagine. I can see why your Prime Minister Cameroon would get a rebellion about this, it is a problem for you guys there. He must himself be fed up with the consequence when he has to ride public transport with those who cannot afford to make this tax and go 'medieval style' about their businesses. Let the ladies have them back!

imelda1969: Please staunch your curious remarks.

<u>challi</u>: Staunch is indeed the word sir, you speak wisely. I may be brief for my reply then, only to say impoverish Britishers must now seize this day to rise up with further steps towards their dignity. Poor little Dutch boy may no more be burden with cruel dike tariffe, but where to take the struggle now siblings?

<u>garethwhy</u>: The mind boggles. You could just end there.

<u>challi</u>: OK, I will say nothing more. Period.

*This is also a Motown band so do not get confused.

SPORTING & GAMES

They have a saying 'Sport and Politicals do not mix'. But Guardian cannot even write a simple article about the sport of hunting one single fox without introducing a politics 'angle' on the whole affair of it. Sometimes a game is just a game. But it is important in this day of ages (approaching midsummer here) to be clear about the moral standing all the same. Speaking for my personal self, I would never go to hunt the fox. I am morally opposing to, and simply cannot bear the thought of, riding the back of an innocent horse while it strains under my gallant weight (94 kilos). If a donkey is available I will consider, otherwise I will sit on a bench and wait happy with a shotgun if this is the only choice. 'Let them come to you' is not a bad philosopher.

"SNP considers voting to stop lifting of foxhunting ban"

In this one is the suggestion of Nicholas Sturgeon to "stand in the way of Tory clamour to repeal legislation" on the hunting of foxmeat.

challi: Really it is not good idea for Mister Sturgeon to stand in a way because he may easily get trampled by horsefoot. There is also big danger the horse must be 'put down' for injury in falling. Health and safety first buddy!

wazza: Bl**dy murdering top-hatted toffs. What ho, old bean! F*** the plebs, f*** the foxes!

challi: I detect your British ironicals, which I like very much! ... If you ever do taste the meat of the fox you will forsure change your mind Wazza. It is best with the herb of the field. Set a big fire in pit in ground with hot stones around fox animal – best to cooking for AT LEAST four hours when you can make a big dancing party. Fine with berrys and horsemilk.

illiterati: Best with herbs?? Foxes have ticks and worms! Tasty yeah?

challi: I am only to assume you never tried the famous Foxtail Soup from Heinz of America? Make yourself to educate so your brain can expand more big.

illiterati: And they are scabrous to boot.

challi: Kindly not to boot poor scabby foxes! They already suffer enough without this kicking when they are down like dogs. Please to make sensible responding or hold your keypad.

everyonesfriend: Illiterati is quite correct: foxes are riddled with all manner of grubs. In a word: inedible.

challi: OK, I am convince. Best then to exterminate these vulgar creature. I will bring cleaving weapon when I come in England to make a good carve-up on their stupid ginger heads.

"Eddie Izzard, marathon man: 'If I can run 26 miles every day, anyone can'"

This was the story of GBLT comedy runner Mister Izzard, who was at this time in the last week of his Sport Relief money-gather in Africa, where he was to run 27 marathons in 27 days! I did not like very much his suggestion however anyone can run themselves a marathon.

challi: My present wife cannot do this, sir. She has wheelchair and frankly this is not a kind of jokey statement I expect from one of your top comedies. She can not even run 1 marathon let alone 27. Do not seek to mock those less fortunate for you are a lucky man with working legs that can run and even dance on the middle night of summer when the moon is at the Zenith in the sky. Do you think my wife will be dancing then? I thought your country was political correct but now I see your real colours when you come to my continent and insult my family.

loveorhate: All marathons nowadays have disabled entrants. I'm afraid your barriers are mental rather than physical. Your treatment of your wife as a hapless victim is of no help, and your outrage at another person's heartfelt attempt to do some good in this world, if I am honest, borders on offensive.

john74: Agree completely. Why not push her chair or walk by her side? Just takes a modicum of initiative.

aliveandkicking: Can't help thinking he must be joking.

challi: Not good though to use the wheelchair on dirt or stones. I expect you are lucky beneficiary of Tar Macadam in your place of habitat. Must I carry my disability lady on my back like a hunch? Not for nearly 27 miles on your nelly sir. It is true though that I have a mental barrier. After bus accident* there is a steel plate in my headbone. (Lucky for me compared to my lady wife however. I do not wish to complain about my own fortune for I have been prosperous a little – have a nice Grundig computerphone where I now make types – and on top of this my up-and-coming wife from online will be a walker for things like the market.)

loveorhate: I think you're missing the point. Apologies, I was under the mistaken impression you knew the background to this article. Mr Izzard is in fact raising money for a charity from the UK – for whom this story is primarily intended. He was merely suggesting that his own feat isn't so extraordinary and that many people could in fact manage a long(ish) run. Taking personal offence does seem somewhat excessive here. The barriers are often in the mind. Maybe your wife and yourself could undertake some form of physical exercise together that takes one or both of you outside your comfort zone(s). At any rate I wish each of you a content and prosperous life.

challi: Thank you for your thoughtful reply. There is a place here by the fire for you during cold nights – the nights for roasted kudu under stars; the nights for music of metals, the nights for woodstomping. 'My butternut is your butternut' is how we say it.

---

*This same bus accident (due to my epileptical cousin Yongu, who was the driver) indeed put my first wife in her small chariot, which is when I came to take up employ at the Freetown T-shirt factory. I am only home by the weekends since then, while she waits in the shed. This will soon change with replacement wife with good Scots legs, and I will take a full leisure arrangement with television and percussions seven days a week. Glad to say for the moment I still catch up with my cousin twice weekly to and from the factory, as he now drives the Freetown route. Fun to listen on his latest mishaps on the roadway – you always come away with a big grin on the face!

"Eddie Izzard tired yet triumphant after running 27 marathons in 27 days"

hoopthemott: Hats off to Eddie, fantastic achievement!

challi: We do not take the hat off in the sun sir. It can give you the mad heat as we say. My neighbour was never to recover. Now he only eats his fingers, and his vocabularies is only one word ('okras', which is what he is now only to mumble all the day).

mistyeyes: I don't think I could run even a single marathon in 27 days.

challi: Are you disable? You can try even in wheelchair, only 1 mile a day to start and bit by bit you do MORE.

mistyeyes: No, I was only joking about my fitness, or lack of! As in, I couldn't come anywhere near to running a marathon :)

challi: This is political incorrect. You must say 'snickers' in these days, not 'marathon' – unless you are backward in the head. Get with the programme man!

"Sky buys exclusive rights to all Formula One"

After Channel 4 broadcasted their first Big Prize race, this was news that Bernie Ecclestone made a future-ahead pay-TV deal – it's progressive man! This will be time to dust off my Matsui and go to fruit stall for new chip-card. In the meantime I had much opinion on the race.

challi: I don't think you can make a better accident than Fernando Alonso last week – upside down and back to front in two hundred miles of an hour. Congratulations for fantastic beginning of Channel 4 race filming and Pirelli sponsors. Bigtime smashup kudos. BBC was never this good. Hopeful Sky can improve even more for benefit of ALL sportfans.

mackieman: Fernando Alonso's accident was not set up so that Channel 4 could claim more exciting coverage than the BBC.

challi: Ah I see, you are on the inside there with Nando's mishap. Say no more man. ;-) Big up that Sky can make best accidents anyway – if you throw right money at the problem you can solve it good and fast.

Rupertman's head is always grand on ideas, find best way to make BIG spectacular. As we like to say, you can put a ribbon on the branch overnight and make it happen. This I will do with ribbon on which I shall write Mclaren team name, which is 'Mclaren'. You will see it come to pass. Always like to watch the Big Prix going round and round in their supercars.

Paragon: "sportfans"?!? Only those who want to shell out for Sky TV for the likes of Murdoch and Ecclestone. Not in a million years. Count me out.

challi: No need for buy satellite man. You can go a bar – I choose the Cool Bar by the bus station as it has confortable seating and I know the manager (he was dirty with my niece one time). There I drink free tapwater with old street trampler we call Stinku, making a laugh on the backsides of these two misters' faces (Murdock and Eccletones, I talk of you!) while they drink their idiot champagnes (way expensive pal, more the fools they are) and eat their caviars and smoky salmons in their big palaces of gold with luxury red sports car parked outside and dolly ladies making frolic around swimming pool in them stupid damn bikini.

"Manchester United v Liverpool: Europa League webchat"

This was a live chat you can join in if the football game you are watching is too boring for your eyeholes.

> <u>challi</u>: Can get this game on TV but not the best match like Barca so I will go to the hanging instead to see the end of a very bad gentleman.

> <u>manusteve</u>: .... yourself!

This Steve was I think a typical football fanatical bred of England. (If he knew what the bad gentleman had done with a horny fruit of the field he would understand my brain.) I was made to reply in a similar kind of fashion and lay down my challenge:

> <u>challi</u>: Sir you speak like the mongrel dog who cannot control his bowels. Come and play real football without shoes and we will have a merry laugh on your British belly and moobies.

> <u>manusteve</u>: Fine mate. Prepare for a horror tackle.

"Neymar leads Barcelona to Champions League final despite Bayern victory"

Indeed I did make a good decision in watching Barcalona the next week at the Cool Bar. There I spied a curious action by the Bayern Munchen manager which may be one of your funny Europan customs or some kind of perversion, I cannot tell.

challi: I was noticing the Mister Guardiola touch the bottomside (not the hole part) of many player and also Barca manager in the match. Is he playing funny game, I do not make heads or tails of it?

victoradams: Come on mate, he was just being friendly with ex colleagues.

challi: I see madam Victoria. Thank you for your illuminations. Still I am not quite to understand properly. Is this the okay way for behaving in a hotel when I make my visit to Europa? Will the manager make a friendly greet of me in this way? Is this the best way to introduce myself to his daughter (assume she is nice-looking for your answer)?

"Gary Neville left Valencia in ignominy – but at least he bit the bullet"

This was tragic article on danger of making play with live ammonitions.

challi: A man should never bite the bullet. You can make it go wonky when you pull the trigger and even sometimes you get an explosion in the barrel. My cousin Olli lost two finger after he used bullets with dents. The bushman got completely away and we were made to go hungry all the weekend.

lordy: LOL. Sir, you are a regrettably-underrated genius!

challi: Lordy dear, I shall take that sentiment to heart. Many lambastings of my content on this site – your comment is a rare and kind exception! If you are ever in Zaita province there shall remain a place by the fireside for you in the balmy evenings and as much s'mbatta-tanni-wazatanaga as a man can eat.

ENVIRO-MENTALS

The end of the world is nigh and there is nothing we can do about it in Zaita. It is up to you Westerners to make a big smoke-sucking machine that will clean the air and stop the whales getting clogged up with plastic supermark bags. When everything goes bang I will go to live down the mine where I can light coals to see ... unless I can make my escape to the high grounds of the Northlands (indeed I write of your very own country, with its fine manners and bright green fields!). My plans are in the actual planning stage. In the meantime I will continue my work at the T-shirt factory where the chimney turns the sky a beautiful browney-orange in the eveningtimes. You can drink a nice beer while you watch the leaves fall off the tree and the yokel people wilt in the heat.

"Does climate change make it immoral to have kids?"

Challiwimbe says 'no'! In the future, everyone will live on Mars for fifteen minutes.

challi: I have made six of the children so far but problem is that six is unlucky number. Also so is seven and eight. So I must go on and make three more. Problem there is if I make it to nine – very lucky number! – but I get unlucky twins in last batch, then I am on ten, which is the most unlucky number of all. Then off I must go again, but big advantage for me is I get to make it stick LOTS of times with a different one.

soitgoes: Wazzock.

challi: Come off your high one man! Too much stigmatize with labels buddy.

"Sea levels set to rise 'far more rapidly than expected'"

Here was a story from Ice Scientists that the melting will be twice as quick as everybody knew. It will get very wet up to your knees if we do not stop smoking the world out.

challi: As it will come to pass like the Costner Prediction and the story of Noah, you will find the seas do rise and the ark she must be builded. Then only can you take the few upon board to make a future when the seas doth subside. I have seen the movie of the future and it is a sad sight with waves washing and breakdown of laws and orders. I would not take two of everything, I would take more – but remember you should not take the brother and sister animals for the offspring born of sinful coupling shall be twisted of face like the people of the village which neither man nor woman nor beast has entered or left in twelve generations. Think on it friends. Do you want this Waterworld for your children? Yank out the ocean plug now! (Metaphor. Do not yank on the real plug.)

"Ben Stokes sees his world collapse after Carlos Brathwaite's T20 blast"

This looks more like a cricket tale for the Sporting section. But inside the article you can see the environment agenda – as just when the Caribbean team scored a big hit with the bat to win the game, "the field was overwhelmed by a tidal wave of West Indian cricketers and staff, men and women."

challi: Terrible to think that this tidal wave struck the poor cricketers just as they claimed their great victory over the Old Empire team. Is this what we have done to our environment with the oceans rising so that the poor West India man must drown on a wave? I bet the whitemen all had lifeboats. I hear that it is the moon that causes these bad tides on us. You can bet you last finger it is time to do something about this.

february2: Different kind of wave. And the moon has nothing to do with it.

challi: I will not listen to this imperialist reversion of the truth. The moon is known here as The Devil of the Tides and we all know EXACTLY how it operates.

february2: Do you think there's some 'man in the moon' pulling levers?

challi: Everybody know this is stupid. There has been no man in the moon since nineteen-seventy-something.

february2: For the literal-minded: it was 1972, Eugene 'Gene' Cernan. First was Armstrong.

challi: With this I will not argue. Louis 'Neil' Armstrong was indeed the first man on the moon – and the first blackman fired into space. He looked down onto Planet Earth, which was very beautiful from up there, and it was then that he said to himself, 'This Is What A Wonderful World'. (He could see the trees of green but the part about the 'red roses too' is a poetical license.*)

february2: I suppose he played the cornet up there too??

challi: This is a complete prepostery: you cannot play the trumpet horn in outer space or even in a space helmet. The tune was made on the return journey when there was nothing else to do. There was a big argument in the cockpit because the horn noises made Mister Aldrin crazy in this confined space, which is how gets the name 'Buzz' because he can still hear the notes ringing in his earholes to this day.

<u>february2</u>: What cr*p!

<u>challi</u>: Excuse me, you should take the encumberance upon yourself to learn your post-colonical studies. Then you will know. Sad story for Mister L Armstrong is that later he must take the rap for drugs on a bicycle, in the Tour of France. Everybody know it was a police fit-up job because he is Afro. (Side-note: trumpet horn *can* be played on a bicycle but that is no use to him now with his ban.)

<u>onlyme</u>: Easy there! Sounds like you've been on the vino!

<u>challi</u>: Vino not available here. I drink the fermented fruit of the twanza tree (we call it 'twannamuti'), following by seven day trance of hunger by the river. Eyes stop rolling day four. If you are lucky like me you get to keep sane.

---

*Louis also saw the Great Wall of China but did not put it in the song because at that time there was a great prejudice in America against the Chinamen, which was called 'communISM'.

ARTISTICS &
CULTURALS

In this part you will be a little bit educated about the differentials we have amid our two cultures: 'here culture', and 'there culture'. You will see mutualistic learning between myself and your providers of content in the comments area. Always you can become a better man if you listen to the others. So shut up and hear what I have to tell you in this section coming.

Later on there will be more liberal exchangements. And like I did explain, things are afoot here. I am very excitable to make my own cultural impression with Britain, which will begin with the formal consuming of the marriage with my web wife. I have nearly enough money for a plane ride now. There is so much to be shared between us! Who knows, you may one day find me grinning right up your very own high street.

"'It has to be hot. It has to be creative': Don Cheadle on his 10-year quest to play Miles Davis"

Jazz Music is nearly as great as Challiwimbe's Metal Music. You can get a good groove going even if your neighbour is too stupid to recognize.

challi: I take a big joy from Mister Cheadle in this film and also from the trumpeting of Mister Miles Davies (who never made it to the moon). But if you want some real good blowing on one you need to get a handle on the big lady of the Cape called Gourdina Mapazatala who makes the best ever noise with her vuvuzela. Open you hearing and dig it man!

philnoodles: Wow, you're cool.

challi: Thank you madam. Gourdina Mapazatala (we say 'Gourdi') rocks it jazztime. You make a dance if you want to.

patdown: The vuvuzela's about as pleasant as electric shock treatment.

challi: You have not seen Gourdina Mapazatala party trick – for sure you will change your face when you learn what it can do.

opencardoor: "Gourdina can make the best ever noise with her vuvuzela" ... Is that a euphemism?

challi: F.I.Y. vuvuzela is horn of the kudu buck – which you take by getting a good ride on his back and make a fast cleaver blow before he does a throw on you. Please be sensible however: it is actual bad luck to take two horns from the same beast. (Leave him some hearing, we say – he may like the jazz too!)

"Turner prize 2015: an end to the same-old same-old. Bring it on!"

This was wrote by an art critical in admiration of the jury for your Turner prize, who want to make the contest more radical after it has become uninteresting like a zebra crap.

<u>challi</u>: In honour of your Turner prize I am today spending my day with one foot in the lavatory bowl and making dolphin noise. Naturally also I must wear hat made of bat dung – or is this not the case? Please advice me wise peoples of developed world so I can become like yours. Also, sock or no sock?

<u>challi</u>: I repeat, sock or no sock? Urgent please.

<u>challi</u>: Foot cold now.

<u>barndoor</u>: The bat dung's optional. Make sure the sock is dangling out of your a***.

<u>challi</u>: Thank you ... I think. I shall now always keep at least one sock up there in case of impromptu street exhibition I like to make. Maybe get some side-money busking like this if I come in Trafalgar Square?

"Matthew McConaughey on The Sea of Trees: 'Anyone has as much right to boo as they do to ovate'"

This was about a film from America that nobody liked.

challi: Good for you western people to take up traditions of motherland you were leaving many thousand years past. We here are often making boo sounds in cinema at local town. Sometimes we throw egg at screen or also tomato. Other time we beat on manager with woods. He learn now to show best movies like Sex And City 2 where I understand much of your customs.

challi: Please note on the ovating however: I understand a lady's right to this if she is in the fertile mood but perhaps it is not best in the cinema (unless maybe back row).

losttheplot: Superb.

"Digital artist Ann Hirsch on why her 'singing vagina' empowers women – and terrifies men"

Why put the ugly parts on display? Do I show you my exit part? You can bet your last finger that Marcel Marceau would be turning in the grave to think on this one. Still two good things were to come of this article: first, as you will not know but now will learn, my pet hyena howls in very good tune when he hears the provincial anthem of Zaita ("Oh bless we men of the bush, we shall strike down the metalman invaders," etc.), so I made good to write immediately to the museum in question to get him a place in this exhibition. And second, I was to find a man of Britain who can make a laugh on things like Challi!!

kingjohn: 'empowers women'? It certainly doesn't. It serves to shame and disenfranchise those poor ladies whose wotsit cannot parp 'Somewhere over the Rainbow'.

challi: Sir, I have some knowledge of the musicals for I am myself a metal banger. This is a good song to test the vaginal cords as it has an octave leap in the chorus part. This leap is a doubling of the frequency–hertz, which means the vaginal cords must vibrate twice as quick as before when going from 'some' to 'where'. Many ladies will struggle with this.

smarties78: Seems they have to crowbar the word 'vagina' into every article these days.

challi: My niece does not use the word 'v----a'. She likes to call it her 'police siren' because everybody can know when she is coming even if she is around the corner. She can empty a room no trouble. I went to the Cool Bar by the bus station and the manager told me to tell her not to come in again because he lost too many customers. If her police siren could talk it would have a LOT of stories to tell but I am glad it can not.

imabeliever: Seems you're not taking this at all seriously.

challi: This is because it is not pleasant of this article to make fun of mental ill people who believe they have a v----a with superpowers in this exhibition. With therapys and educations you can help the victim learn the proper use for EVERY part of the body. Start with 'feet are made for walking' and progress slowly - but ALWAYS with a licensed head doctor in supervision of these types.

"Ronnie Corbett dies aged 85"

Here was a sad article about one member of a comedy trio called The Three Ronnies, who passed away the day before. There is only one left now and his name is McDonald.

challi: Very nice man. Indeed also his wife was a very good gymnastical lady in her time much adorned with medals.

eastiseast: Flimsy.

challi: Thank you.

taffetta: That was Olga *Korbut.*

biginstrument: Whooooooosh!

challi: Taffetta, this must be a communist spelling? ... Anyway you can see her video online. Search for over 15 and enjoy! (Remember to pull blind down please.)

"Tom Hardy, Tom Hiddleston, Idris Elba ... who should be the next James Bond?"

This was a silly argument about who should get Daniel Craig's tuxedo when he has finished with it. Give it up to charity man!

andypandy: Isn't about time we had a female Bond?

challi: We have here a fine actress named Shonia M'Stibhane, who has featured in many good films (including Deadly Chop-Up 1, 2, 3 AND 4). She has a scarred face to increase looking 'hard' so perfect for Bond. Also she has good muscles as her ancestors practised by habit the famous 'Lion Run' in Zaita province, gaining a very strong bloodline – as your own Charles Darwin was to prove in his Evolution Theory of Fittest and Fastest. (You can evolve in half a second when you spy a lion on your back-end.)

sanitypersonified: Idris Elba, no contest.

challi: Indeed a contest would be vulgar! I would not like to see one because if these guys get in a fight normally Tom Hardy would win easy – or him and the other Tom might gang up on Mister Elbow. Please Britain, no contest for Bond.

<u>pterodactyl</u>: Elba's good for me. Or Dominic West?

<u>challi</u>: You cannot choose one with silly hair. It may be straight, maybe a bit wavy, but not curly like a clown. I want to see Nicholas Sturgeon as Bond with his tough accent, scary features and eyes like flints (which are stones you can mine here if you can afford an electric clattahammer). Anyway Idris Ebola might not be available as there is a new multistory car park opening in our town and I have written an invite for him to make it open with scissors*.

*Stop pressing please! I may not be there to greet him. Big plans are underway in my life circumstances.

LAST THINGS

My plans are coming forward – progressively of course. I am stepping into the now. In fact I will soon be a full-fledged contemporaneous migrant in Britain, with my hotwife of the 'net. My heart is indeed singing! And there is a warm feeling in my loins that shall before long be sated.

My ticket is booked for travel (yes!) and my new wife awaits me with open arms and legs. I may like to settle in Croydon-upon-Thames, where it is warmer than Scotland – if my good lady will go 'south of the border' as she says it (this is not a sex comment). My sticks and pipe and percussion drums are packed to go. I will take the corrugated iron from the neighbour's roof on the morning of my flight. Tomorrow is the actual day my friends! The pilot is polishing his proverbial propellors, and wild zebras could not drag me away. The residentials of the United Kingdom will get to learn something of Zaita culture when I play my metal music as the crickets chirp and moon rises every night above the beautiful bushy landscape of Croydon. So much have I to impart for your good learning – and verce-visa too. Let us modernize it progressive-style! Let us join in one-being! May our holes be greater than the sums of our parts. Yet always viva the differentials that make us special. Together, comrades, we can do it different.

So now it is here. The time when I must say 'cheerio' – and thank you for reading my book. I hope you enjoyed it even more than me. Goodbyes are so cruel. Let us call it *au reservoir*, rather than farewell, as it is always sad to be losing touch. I will be back on the web – do not worry! Indeed you can get me with a tweet if you like (@challiwimbe). Or you may catch up with my face in your very own country when I arrive. And please always remember, when things go bad and you are at your lowest point – with a liver disease, or the curse of a thousand Bushmen upon your soul, or terrible problems of the brain like a man started banging on your head with a cricket bat and forgot to stop – don't forget to make a laugh on it man!!!

Acknowledgings

Thank you to my Scottie wife, Brunnhilda, for her nonstop encouraging in my earholes. And to my original wife for eBaying her wheelchair to help pay plane ticket to UK.

Big shout-up for Chairperson of Grundig – in way of thank yous, I am posting a jar of fermented twanza juice. Expect customs fee your end. (Health and safety note: on no account shake before opening. Toxic only to rats.) Would appreciate new battery by return – <u>model B700</u>.

Proof

Made in the USA
Charleston, SC
15 May 2016